Still Learning At 90 Years

Still Learning At 90 Years

ReadersMagnet, LLC

Stella Kerkvliet

Still Learning At 90 Years
Copyright © 2019 by Stella Kerkvliet

Published in the United States of America
ISBN Paperback: 978-1-949981-48-3
ISBN eBook: 978-1-949981-49-0

All rights reserved. No part of this publication may be reproduced, stored in a retrieval system or transmitted in any way by any means, electronic, mechanical, photocopy, recording or otherwise without the prior permission of the author except as provided by USA copyright law.

The opinions expressed by the author are not necessarily those of ReadersMagnet, LLC.

ReadersMagnet, LLC
10620 Treena Street, Suite 230 | San Diego, California, 92131 USA
1.619.354.2643 | www.readersmagnet.com

Book design copyright © 2019 by ReadersMagnet, LLC. All rights reserved.
Cover design by Ericka Walker
Interior design by Shemaryl Evans

For Me

Love independent of time,

Countless like the grains of sand,

Endless as the heavens,

Hope in this torn land.

Print this indelible word,

On my tormented soul.

Carve it in my heart,

Make it only my goal.

Teach me to know this love,

With every bit of me,

Peel the scales from my eyes,

That this imperfect soul might see.

Replenish my starving heart,

With your wisdom and healing love,

Give me strength and patience,

Heal this heart so numb.

Snow

Walking through the snow,

It falls upon my face.

Wind and snow upon my hair,

Like a veil of lace.

I forget my cares,

My worries disappear,

In a magic world of white,

When there are no tears.

Lying on my lashes,

Like a lover's kiss,

Mine is a quiet happiness,

In the snow like this.

Mother

I've seen the beauty of her smile,
Felt the comfort of her arms,
The gentle twinkle in her eyes,
The rapture of her charms,
Something in her seems to glow
Like a warming light,
Someone I can go to,
Because she seems so right.
In her I've found,
What I have envied others,
Something very precious,
Someone called a mother.

Absolution

Sorrow rends my heart

In a throbbing, deep refrain,

So sinful, and unworthy

A deep and hurting pain.

Heart and soul so full,

Brings a searching quest,

A yearning for forgiveness,

To still this dark unrest.

The comfort comes from God,

"Go and sin no more,"

Take your mother's hand.

She'll lead you to my door.

Kneeling at the rail,

The whole world seems to shine,

God will love and keep me,

Peace will soon be mine.

Charley

The day was cold and still,

When to our steps he came,

Shivering, cold and sick.

A puppy tired and lame.

Unknown age and breed,

Yet his blood was royal blue,

His love and devotion endless,

No human was so true.

He protected children all,

loved beyond human kind,

Neglected not his charge,

Can you say as much of a man?

He was known just as Charley,

Showed delight

With guarded care,

For those who might offend.

Oh, how he would beg,

When he thought he'd displeased,

One of his beloved humans.

How his eyes would grieve.

It seems I still see him,

Leap with joyous glee,

Snow piled on his nose,

Memories dear to me.

A ball was always near,

He'd watch and beg to play.

Running, prancing, laughing,

Enjoying each glorious day.

He knew whom to doubt

And the smile would leave his eyes,

The growl would thunder deep,

Trusting not man's lies.

Now our time has come,

To grieve for our beloved friend,

He can't be replaced or forgotten,

And broken hearts to mend.

Yet I cannot help but wonder,

At the heartlessness of one,

Who deliberately took his life,

Does he know what he has done?

Gary

Tall & proud,

With head held high,

Arms outstretched,

To the windswept sky.

My oldest son,

With heart of pure gold,

Born in this time,

But the oldest of souls.

Always there for me,

No matter the task,

With brother and sisters,

He placed himself last.

This child so precious,

As all children are,

Born with soul,

Ageless by far.

I thank God for him,

Each day and night,

Could not do without him,

A world without light.

Just Wondering

Sometimes I sit alone,
And watch the silent sky,
What secrets does it hold,
Does it ever lie?

Count the sparkling stars,
Wonder at their light,
Windows of Heaven,
Candles so bright.

The moon seems suspended,
Like some giant ball,
Orange, cold and quiet,
Guardian of us all.

The dawn so slow in coming,
With a stealthy glow,
My questions still unanswered,
Something we'll never know.

Dona

The beauty of her tousled head,

Those shining, brilliant eyes,

Full of mischief, sparkling,

Blue as the bluest skies.

Just like a golden lily,

Petals to unfold,

Dainty and so lovely.

Heart and soul like gold.

Such a tiny, little girl,

Her arms lifted high,

"Mommy, how I love you".

Just like the breezes sigh.

She's like a fairy dancing,

In some sunlit glade

She's my babe daughter,

This lovely little maid.

True To Yourself

Be true to yourself,

Your own heart don't betray,

This motto I live by,

Each and every day,

When things seem too much,

And you feel you can't go on,

Look deep into your heart,

Peace like the golden song.

True unto yourself,

Endless as eternity.

Peace in heart and soul.

Deep as the silent sea.

Carol

So like a lovely autumn leaf,
Of brown, and green and gold,
Gentle as a newborn fawn,
She's goodness to behold.
Her eyes so soft and green,
Shines with a special light,
Tenderness personified,
Beyond most human sight.
She thinks about God's creatures.
God has blessed her greatly,
With something very rare.
She is so like a hymn,
For which she was named,
Soft as muted music,
Carol is her name.

Silver Song

The silver song of rain,

A million glittering jewels,

Freely dropping where they may,

Only answers nature rules.

A violet's lifted face,

The rain a lover's kiss,

Bends and spreads her purple skirt,

Blooming in her bliss.

The silver song has ended,

Until another day,

Leaves as its grand finale,

Rainbows, midst golden rays.

Bernie

My all American boy,
Freckles by the score.
Teasing, laughing, blue eyes,
Who could ask for more.
Band-aids here and there
From falling from a tree.
Playing with his friends,
But always back to me.
A frog beneath his bed,
Baseball bat and glove,
A broken clock needs fixing,
Mechanics are his love.
But when the twilight comes,
The teasing eyes are quiet,
"Mom, how much I love you"
Everything seems right.

Dream Alone

Let me dream my dreams alone,

As I have always done,

Dreams of that which might have been,

Like rainbows in the sun.

I dream the magic of your smile

Of things I wish I could be,

I know the love lite in your eyes,

Will never be for me.

For I was born to dream alone,

From outside looking in,

But oh my dear, my love for you,

Goes beyond all kith and kin,

Someday, I know you'll find a love.

My dreams and prayers for you,

Are for your happiness, old dear,

Your dreams, my prayers come true.

Solitude

Solitude is my dream,

Soothing, comforting peace.

To meditate in silence,

Heartache and sorrow cease.

Solitude, ah, I feel,

The touch of a blessed hand.

In comfort and forgiveness.

A prayer for this torn land.

The Lonely Years

The years have passed so swiftly,

I've wondered where they went.

My heart aches so softly,

Wondering—what they've meant.

The days, the months, the years,

Swiftly tumbling by.

Someday there'll be an end,

In my silent cry.

Anger

They rage with the wind,

As one kindred soul

Welcome the fury,

As we play out the role.

A wild angry giant,

His wrath, unappeased,

Breaking, destroying,

Forcing all to their knees.

They weep with a wail,

A deluge of sorrow,

An outpouring of pain,

Tis gone-'tis all gone,

And nothing is gained.

"The Depth Of Love"

The depth of love is boundless,

Beyond our wildest dreams.

A brilliant yielding splendor,

Blinding as the sun bright beams.

Too many hearts made narrow

Through self-centered pride.

Too many hearts are selfish.

Too many hearts have lied.

Love is the core of giving,

Of placing someone first.

Love is understanding.

Love is a quenchless thirst.

Love is sweet and gentle.

Love is wild and free.

Love makes life worth living.

Love is for eternity!

Whispering

The whispering ghosts of yesterday,

Watch with hated breath.

Dreams composed of fantasy,

Foreseeing their painful death.

I seem to feel their shadows,

Know a friendship with their loss,

Remember a life before me,

Where they carried their lonely cross.

A cross composed of loneliness,

Of pain and bitter woe,

One embraced at last freely,

One I'll always know.

A Speck Of Dust

Oh -to be a speck of dust,

To lie beneath your feet,

To feel your gentle footsteps

My happiness complete.

To be consumed within your heart,

Until I am no more,

There's nothing more I wish to be.

I ask, beg, implore.

To know your gentle hands,

Clay-like me to mold,

Accept whatever you might wish,

My imperfect soul to keep and hold.

There's nothing in this world,
Compared to what may be,
To carve the scales from off my heart,
That my soul might see.

Unwieldy tongue, I can't express,
But the yearning grows and grows,
To be your little speck of dust,
To belong to you, and know.

The Sentence

Three men of equal fame and wealth.
Stood before the judgment throne,
To answer for their years on earth,
To answer and atone.

One man spoke of pride,
Selfishness and shame
Of lying and slander,
T'was how he gained his fame.

Another spoke of hardship,
Of bitterness and strife.
He spoke with hidden meaning,
Midst this, he lived his life.

The third one stood with downcast head,
His whispered word was low.
I've gathered neither wealth nor fame,
Love is all I know.

Intangible

Intangible and hidden,
Unable to define,
Sometimes unacceptable,
By prides indelible line.

Some take it for granted,
Others never know,
That fleeting as a shadow,
It could come and go.

Some use it to hurt,
To hurt and then betray,
Beaten, soiled and trod upon,
Then starts a slow decay.

Once known it is precious,
Once lost it's not regained,
Sad that this greatest blessing,
Should be destroyed and maimed.

Perhaps now you wonder,

This thing of which I write,

An elusive of which I write,

An elusive thing called love,

That can vanish overnight.

The Answer

I gaze into a pool,
And see reflection there,
Shadows of life,
Often filled with dark despair.

I see someone praying,
Hope a flickering dream,
The pool would cloud and darken,
Her ears were closed it seemed.

Prayers aren't always answered,
As we would will it so,
God answers in wisdom,
Sometimes He must say no!

Someday the pool may brighten,
As crystal as a mirror,
The darkness will all vanish,
His answer will be clear.

Hidden Self

I see hidden self,

A being–wild and free,

Hear this rebel heart of mine,

Sing–on dancing trees.

Oh, how I glory all alone,

The drums of a soul at peace,

Joyous softly beating,

Happiness released.

This world inside is endless,

Limitations not for me,

I challenge mediocrity.

My hidden self is free!

The Door

Decay and mold the suit
The earth the shroud of death.

The spring the morning room,
The wind the only breath.

'Tis my only love.
Alive, alas no more.

I search and wonder, lost,
I knock at Heaven's door.

Searching

This eve I sit and listen,
To the voices of my world.
Turbulent, seeking, questing,
Searching arrows hurled.

Am I blinded to the truth?
I want, I need to know!
Is mine a barren soul or
Am I my deadliest foe!

Is my fear born of confusion,
Bred in a stupid mind?
Cringing, self-protection
Afraid to face and find!

Do I hide behind my pride,
Destroying my will to live?
A life complete with dignity,
Have I forgotten how to give!

My soul is tired and weary.
I beg for truth and courage–okay
To accept, and then atone.

Dreamless Sleep

Loneliness is mine,

No matter where I go,

This cross sometimes so heavy,

I accept it so.

Oh—the lonely hours,

At times so dark and deep,

Soon fade and vanish,

In my dreamless sleep.

The Plea

Love independent of time,

Countless as grains of sand,

Endless as the heavens,

Hope in this torn land.

Print this indelible word,

On my tormented soul.

Carve it in my heart,

Make it my only goal.

Teach me to know this love,

With every bit of me,

Peel the scales from my eyes,

That this imperfect soul might see.

Replenish my starving heart,

With your wisdom and healing love,

Give me strength and patience,

Heal this heart so numb.

The Landlord

To dwell in golden grandeur,

Has never been my dream,

To trod the path of fortune?

A prison it would seem.

This home where "I live"

Within my soul to keep

Its young arms enfold me,

Hold me, warm and deep.

I'll guard my home from ruin,

Because He dwells within,

The landlord of my being,

The man from Galilee.

The Coin

She's with me as a shadow,
Knows all I do and think,
In tune with every footstep,
This shy and shadowed link.
And yet I know her not
Am I afraid to try
To meet and understand her?

So, my fears, I justify,
I see both sides of the coin,
One savage, wild and free
Self-seeking proud and lonely,
Both sides, I know are me.

The Cross

I find no evil in her heart;
I find no discontent.
I find acceptance of the cross,
And the pain, that was sent.

I see her human failings,
I see them one and all,
I fight with silent fury,
When she stumbles and falls.

Don't Question

God has always blessed me,
Watched me day and night,
Given me what's best for me,
When doubt has dimmed my sight.

Sometimes I used to wonder,
Now I never do.
His ways are often hidden,
This I've learned 'tis true.

I used to ask the question,
"Please, dear God why?
The answer comes within my heart,
It will never lie.

There always is a reason,
Though hidden it may be.
It's not for me to question,
Not for me to see.

A Hymn

Millions of voices in song,

Sung in the silence of time.

Chorus of infinite glory,

The artist of beauty sublime.

Hear the cry of the blue jay,

Rapidly chatters the squirrel,

Busily lining each moment,

Caring not for people's mad whirl.

There! The voice of the robin,

Fluted song of silver and gold,

The drum of the gentle bullfrog,

A symphony heard o'er the world.

The wind, the strings of the harp,

Fingers of angels to play,

A song of peace and his comfort,

The end of a beautiful day.

The Golden God

Power! Oh yes.

I will be king

With a fist of iron.

Of my glory, they'll sing.

The men who loved

For glory and gold

Take all they could get

They gambled and lost their souls.

Peace

Dreams were to be broken,
When life at last we face.

And see it's no dream in a garden,
No picture of roses and lace.

Once I dreamt of a love,
A love gentle and deep.

Then I woke, my dream shattered,
Can you see a heart silently weeps?

For mine was a dream in a mist,
A ream long faded and gone.

Yet, a strange peace in my soul,
Though I still remember and long.

Atonement

Head bowed in sorrow,

Rejected and alone,

Agonized and bleeding,

Our sins to atone.

Agony personified,

Etched in every line,

On the cross suspended,

Eternity is thine.

The Breath

The breath of thy fingers,

Comes as a gentle sigh,

Touched with tender longing,

Then falls away and lies.

Hopeless, yearning heart,

That dares no more to dream.

Wistful, watching, waiting,

For nothing is what it seemed.

Uncertainty

So many people all around,
But so alone I feel.
Never quite belonging,
True friends are never real.

So afraid to trust,
That someone might betray,
The shyly offered friendship,
That I might be in the way.

Please, dear God, I pray,
Take this uncertainty away.
Give confidence in God and man,
And friends to fill my days.

Men's Greed

I've heard the children of the world,
Heard their hungry cries.

Listened to the words of man,
Heard the greedy lies.

Mothers holding their baby,
Next to a shriveled breast.

Listen, oh please listen,
Shame them in their quest.

Silent World

The forests still and dark,
I walk without aim 'nor rhyme,
Searching for an answer,
That will still this heart of mine.

The silence sweet and deep,
Now broken by a song,
Of a trilling meadowlark,
A muted, golden song.

Wind whispering through the trees,
Playing a plaintive lullaby,
Soothes a lonely heart,
Sings, moans and sighs.

Enchantment is mine,
'Neath green velvet aisles,
I walk in time, suspended,
This world's endless miles.

My footsteps wander on,

I wish forever more,

The timeless stillness of the trees,

This world, another door.

The Artist

Exquisite agony,

Oh pain, joy entwined,

Wrung from my throbbing heart,

Leaves all else behind.

The hands that mold the clay,

Agony supreme,

I yield, and say no more,

The sculpture knife is keen.

The chisel, blade and brush,

To dig, to cut and mold,

Will sculpt a perfect piece,

'Twas long ago foretold.

The chisel gouges deep,

Blackened stain removed,

The seeds of grace are sown,

Fill each fertile groove.

Sensitive fingers carve soul's piece,

Healing leaps to life,

A worthy masterpiece.

At last, the brush of love,

Applied with angel wings,

Shimmering colors pure,

I give all to my king.

Freedom

My heart is crying bitter tears,

For this great and glorious land,

To see the hate and discontent,

To hear our country damned.

Our country stands for freedom

For justice and for good,

Our fathers lived and died for this,

They knew and understood.

I seem to see these gallant men,

Amazement on each face,

Listen to the protests,

This now divided race,

Peace, they scream.

Non-violence is our code,

Then they march,

They smash and curse,

So goes the mocking ode.

Let the reds do as they will,

Our land is great and strong.

Let our neighbors fight alone,

To help cannot be wrong.

Let them fight for freedom,

Small though they may be,

They've fought for oh so many years,

Blind fools!! Their eyes can't see.

One redeeming factor,

Our heritage is strong,

Some of our brave and loyal boys,

Have gone to right the wrong.

They'll help these brave small people,
They'll give their hearts and blood,
Help them gain their freedom,
Some in graves of mud.

The evil, slowly creeping,
It stifles, chokes and kills,
It demands our lives, hopes and dreams,
Countries its maw to fill.

None of us like violence,
But freedom's price comes high,
We must help our fellow man,
Or our country lives a lie.

The Way

A torture twisted path,
Of thorns and razor stones,
A bleeding torn heart,
Lost—but not alone.

Words, a lance to wound,
Laugh, to live a lie,
A wall to lock inside,
To hide a longing cry.

A spirit pressed in clay
Wings, broken, hurt and bent,
Weakened, ebbing strength,
Ask, then grace is sent.

A light of brilliant gold,
Seen with soul not eyes,
The fall of clinging clay.
The path is turning yet, twisted,
Ah, my guide His loving eyes,

I follow, kneel, adore.

A hymn sung by the Word,

Thanksgiving fills my soul.

There–felt but unseen,

At last, free and whole.

Crosses gathered close,

Lead by wisdom more than mine.

To wipe the tears of blood,

From his weary saddened eyes,

By acts of trust and love,

By deeds, not troubled sighs.

Worldly cares aside,

No fear what you may think,

He presses to my soul,

His grace, fulfilling drink.

The thorns and stones,

Still there, I know, but never mind,

To know, and walk with Thee,

Earth's pleasure n'er can bind.

The chains of my heart,

Strength, forged of snow white love,

My God, my master judge,

The Holy Spirit, my love.

Crosses

Life is sad, it's been said,
So many pains and woes,
Worries, cares and trials,
An so the story goes.

One cross might be poverty,
Another one of gold,
Your neighbors might be one of pain,
Each one has been foretold.

If you are so blessed,
To have a cross He gives,
Carry it with loving smiles,
In eternity you'll live.

And yet there are other crosses,
We fail to recognize.
The ones we fashion all alone,
The ones that we devise.

One of these is selfishness,

Charity, unknown.

This heart is dry and hard,

This person walks alone.

This door is rusted shut,

The pain grows through the years.

Love and tenderness are lost,

Bitter, selfish tears.

Another cross is pride,

It knows not how to take,

The honest help of God and man,

So it builds His fate.

This and many others,

Lead to the worst despair,

This one steals our knowledge,

Of one who truly cares.

Despair is turning from Him,
Of shutting Him outside,
We place ourselves above Him,
We gain the sin of pride.

Just take the cross He gives,
His footsteps follow well,
Lease pride despair and selfishness,
This barren road is hell.

Dreams

I see your young exuberance,
To conquer all in life,
Clear-eyed with the joy of living,
Innocent of strife.

Your thought are filled with dreams,
Of love, perhaps of fame,
Of power, gain and fortune,
You're sure 'twill be the same.

Your eyes see a long life,
And all you want to be,
Someone to walk the path with,
What else do you see?

For some he'll choose crosses,

To mold and draw to Him,

With the years you will learn,

Human love can dim.

Child, learn to love, I beg you!

Your joy in another time,

Not in this life of sorrow,

His promise will be thine.

Remember To Know

Have I lost the sight,
To see each perfect thing,
That makes up this world,
Created by my King.

When did I last listen,
To each lovely, golden note,
Of nature's perfect music,
The greatest ever wrote.

Have I lost my feeling,
For my unseen fellowman,
To see my brother in him,
To help in all I can.

No 'tis just at times,

The world throws its sheen,

Of gloss and worldly trails,

On selfishness we lean.

When we forget to kneel,

Forget whose gifts they are,

Then to our knees we come,

And know just what we are.

The Questions

What is this restless stirring,
That twists and gnaws inside?
What is this craving, yearning?
The truth, I've tried to hide.

The past lies dead, forgotten,
Oh no, the memories stay.
The lessons learned, remembered,
Are part of every day.

What are they all about,
These pictures from the past?
Mistakes, joys and sorrows,
How long does heartache last?

Does it last forever,
Until the clay is cold?
Is it my own desires,
That clutch me in their hold?

Or is it in my power,

To yield, and forget the dream.

To live again in His sacred love,

My starving heart redeemed.

'Tis hard to watch and know,

Perhaps, to wonder why?

To walk alone and ponder,

And try to still my cry.

I think my fruitless search,

Followed a human way.

I'll train my restless heart,

God's love, will fill my days.

The Choice

His cross was tall and barren,
Agony supreme,
Writhing tortured body,
All for our sins, it seems.

For each sin committed,
The nails go deeper still,
Ungrateful human soul,
His love for us fulfilled.

He's here watching, waiting,
His arms outstretched to me,
To forgive love and comfort,
Ask and you will see.

Our lives so lonely, empty,
Existence in a void.
He's waiting for His promise,
To take your soul inside.

How many try to live without,

His loving guiding hand,

How many walk alone and lost,

"Ner seem to understand."

Despair and pride walk hand and hand,

The devils tools 'tis true.

Place our souls at the Master's feet

Strength, He'll give to you

His love is greater than the world,

His love encompasses all,

For we, His wayward children,

Must answer to His call.

Our will was given freely,

To each and everyone,

We walk with Him, or turn aside,

Which life have you began?

www.ingramcontent.com/pod-product-compliance
Lightning Source LLC
LaVergne TN
LVHW020436080526
838202LV00055B/5213